Creative
accents
home décor ideas with glass

Fun & Exciting Home Décor
decorating ideas with glass centerpieces

by Robert Zollweg

Designed and written by Robert Zollweg
Photography by Rick Luettke, www.luettkestudio.com
Graphics by Gary Raschke and Robert Zollweg
Art Direction by Gary Raschke

Library of Congress Cataloging-in-Publication Data:

Creative Accents,
Home Decor Ideas with Glass
by Robert Zollweg

www.zollwegart.com

ISBN 978-0-615-57691-6

Printed in the United States of America
By: R. R. Donnelley and Company

I'd like to dedicate this book to my mother,

Virginia Katherine Murphy Zollweg

and to my kids, Rhonda and Doug, Christopher and Sandy
and all their children:
Kaylie, Andrew, Bret, Morgan and Korrin
To Steve Tester, Elaine and Tom Bender, Richard and Sandra Zollweg
Judy and Carl Sims, all their families
and to Annie, my little girl.

There are so many people to thank for making this book a reality.

Gary Raschke, I could not have made it happen without his help.
He has been their every step of the way.
And to Bill Muzzillo's great literary skills.

Jessica Adler, Jane Goble, Jeff Joyce,
Karen Barentzen, Beth Baroncini, Cathie Logan, Denise Grigg,
Kelly Kelley, Gina Baccari, Tom Fratantuono, Roger Williams,
Serena Williams, Vicki Richardson, Amy Lewarchik, Greg Pax,
Brooks Clayton, Natalie Brunner, Sandy Shultz, Brionna Richmond,
Melissa Fleig, Fran Breitner, Ericka Sabo, Rosie Jordan,
Joe Mefferd, Brenda Bennett and Pete Kasper.

And to Libbey Glass, for giving me the opportunity to do what I enjoy doing.

Table of Contents

Introduction

Creative Accents is a special little book that is all about the fun ways you can use glassware around your home or as centerpieces in your home. I'll try to cover as many of the different uses and the times of year when you can change these glass pieces to help decorate for each of these special holidays. I'll also give you some fun and different ideas for the bride and her wedding reception or bridal shower.

Creative Accents is also about presentation. Most of the ideas can be made for just a few dollars and will not take very long to put together. Some may cost a little more, depending on what type of materials you use. I've added some little nuances here and there to spice them up and add a little pizzazz. Grouping them together is what great home decor is all about. I love to group several shapes together and make a more unusual arrangement.

Decorating at home can be as simple as fresh flowers in a vase or a pillar candle on a candle holder, or as elaborate as arranging several pieces together with multiple candles and glass containers. Either way, decorating your home will help brighten your day.

Whether you are a crafter or just someone who wants to make your home a little more beautiful, **Creative Accents** will help you to accomplish some of these decorating ideas and special moments.

Working in the tabletop industry has been very rewarding and where I have learned so much about entertaining. I love to entertain and I hope that **Creative Accents** will be a great way for you to turn your home into some place very special.

Enjoy !

Robert

glassware and materials needed

The following pages will show you some wonderful glass items for making great centerpieces. There are many more different styles of glass in the marketplace that will work just as well as the ones I will discuss and show. I'll give you a few easy ideas on the materials you will need and some tips on putting it all together.

There is really no hard and fast rule on what's right or wrong, good or bad when it comes to decorating your home. It's all up to you and your individual taste. I'll give you a few tips and examples to make it easier for you to look like a professional and make your home a little bit more beautiful.

glassware

On the following four pages are some of the glass containers I use to show some of these ideas for centerpieces and home decor items. There are so many more wonderful pieces of glass that can be used to fill and decorate your home. Use your imagination. Mix it up. Be creative! With all the cool glass pieces in today's marketplace, the possibilities are endless. The containers used in this publication can be purchased from various area retailers.

centerpiece vases

cylinder
vases

15

materials needed

There are endless possibilities when it comes to all the items you can use to fill or decorate these glass containers. Some are as simple as a few glass marbles and a 3" pillar candle or others could be applying or covering each glass item with fabric, ribbon or appliques. I've collected quite a few different fillers from various craft stores just to show you some of the options. Be creative, collect all kinds of things from nature, from memorabilia, your favorite junk collection. Almost anything will work.

Some of the simple tools you will need are:
   a standard hot melt glue gun
   glue sticks
   two sided scotch tape
   regular scotch tape
   scissors
   lots of various candles
   various fillers and craft supplies
   white glue
   wire cutters

The following few pages will show some of the materials you will need. I've purchased them from various craft stores or in craft departments.

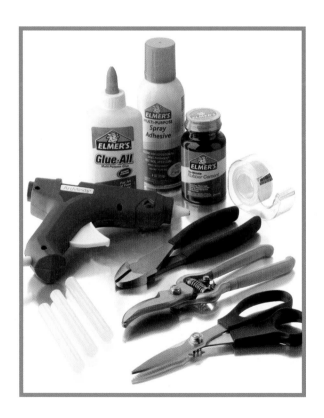

artificial flowers & decorations

decorative
ribbons

natural
vase
fillers

decorative fruit fillers

candle accents

21

wedding & bridal accessories

glass gems
and stones

everyday centerpieces

pedestal bowl

This beautiful centerpiece bowl can be filled with almost anything. I've filled it with water and added some floating gerber daisies. But you can use home decor wooden balls, some glass colored marbles with a candle, pine cones, holiday ornaments, sea shells, glass eggs, almost anything that fits your home decor.

pink passion

Materials needed:
3 different sizes of cylinder vases, 3 hanging votive holders, 3 candle votives and various filling materials.

square vase trio

angela vases

This grouping uses natural stones and ivory candles. You can make this with almost any color scheme to fit your home decor.

Materials Needed:
3 different sized hurricane vases, 3 - 3" pillar candles, some natural colored stones or gravel.

cylinder trio

Materials needed:
3 different sizes of cylinder vases,
one bag of colored glass chips or
sea glass,one bag of natural stones,
one large bag of natural colored
potpourri and a large candle votive.

trumpet vase

This vase is ideal for fresh cut flowers or as a candle holder.

It looks great on a mantle with candles or on a table with fresh flowers.

by the sea

Materials needed:
One 13" round platter, one large cylinder vase, about 3-4 cups of beach sand or gravel, a bag of sea shells, small bag of sea gravel and one 3" x 6" pillar candle.

spring daisies

This is a little crafty but worth the effort. You will need: 3 cylinder vases, various silk flowers on a wire stem, 3 round 4" foam balls, one yard of decorative ribbon.

Cut the stems of the silk flowers at about 2" and stick them, one at a time, into the foam ball until the entire ball is covered with flowers. The more flowers you use the more finished it will look.
Cut the ribbon in a length to fit around the vase. Attach it to the vase with some glue or two-sided tape.
Place the floral ball on top of each cylinder vase and you are ready to go.

salsa trio

This trio centerpiece can be filled with almost anything to fit your home decor. In this display, I've used bright colors for a jazzy latin look.

Materials needed:
3 cylinder vases, 4 - 6" glass saucers or plates, 4 - 3" x 3" pillar candles (orange, red and magenta colored) various silk flowers, enough to fill all three vases, colors to coordinate with candles.

flare footed bowl

This particular footed glass bowl can be used for a variety of things. It's great for centerpieces with candles, but can also be used for potpourri, floating fresh flowers or even as a serving dish for your favorite summer salad.

bubble ball trio

This Bubble Ball Trio works great almost any time of the year. You can fill the bottom of each bubble ball with a variety of fill items.

Materials Needed:
3 bubble balls, 3 hanging votive holders, 3 - 2" votive candles, various fillers to fill the bottom.

big bubble ball

This large bubble ball can be filled with many varieties of decorative types of fillers. Add a candle if you would like.

Materials needed:
one 6" or 8" bubble ball, one glass candle votive holder, one small candle votive, one bag of decorative stones, large bag of sea shells, pine cones, silk flower petals, etc.

candle cascade

Arrange the votives on a plate as shown in the photos. Add the candle votives and scatter a few marbles, stones or glass chips around the glass votives.

Materials needed:
1 - 13" square platter,
4 - 3.5" square glass votives,
4 small candle votives and
one bag of colored
glass chips.

magic lantern

I call this centerpiece the "Magic Lantern," because when you light the candle votive, it will illuminate and sparkle beautifully.

Materials needed:

one 8" wide cylinder vase, one 6" narrow cylinder vase, one candle votive and enough silk flower blooms to fill the container.

potpourri candelabra

Materials needed:
2 tall cylinder vases, 1 short bowl, 3 glass dishes, 3 pillar candles and beautiful rich colored potpourri.

harbour hurricanes

Nothing is more natural than a collection of sand and sea shells. Some sand, seashells, old drift wood and a couple of beautiful natural colored candles are all that you need to complete this picturesque centerpiece.

41

wedding & bridal centerpieces

weddings: summer, spring, winter or fall

I've put together the following ideas for weddings and bridal shower centerpieces using an all white color scheme, but all of them can be adapted to your own color scheme. Simply change the color of the candles, marbles or any accessories to your theme color. It's that simple and all your own.

Fresh flowers are always wonderful, but sometimes they are either out of your budget or out of season. So artificial flowers work wonderfully. They last forever and your guests can take them home.

Using any simple vase or footed hurricane filled with beautiful spring fresh or silk flowers makes a wonderful centerpiece for your table at either the bridal shower or wedding reception. Candles are always a wonderful accent to a centerpiece. Some places do not allow real candles with an open flame, so look into the battery operated candles or votives.

Another small tip that I always tell the bride and groom: "Be creative, and try to put a personal touch on everything. This is your day and it needs to reflect you, not your wedding coordinator, your mother or your sister. Each of you knows what you want your special day to be, so let it show."

precious petals

This is one of my favorites - simple, beautiful yet very affordable. The flowers, candle and glass pieces can be of any color to coordinate with your color scheme.

Materials needed:
one 10" glass garden vase, one small hurricane vase, one - 3" x 3" white pillar candle, various white silk or fresh flowers, two cups of clear and white glass marbles or glass chips.

candelabra trio

What a beautiful centerpiece in the center of a round table at your reception!

Materials needed:
3 cylinder vases, 3 saucer dishes, 3 - 3" pillar candles, large bag of silk flower buds or silk flowers.

adorn candle trio

Beautiful, white lacy ribbon adds a whole new dimension to these plain candle holders. Take a piece of ribbon and cut it to fit around each of the adorn hurricanes. Glue or tape together. Place the pillar candle in the center of each. Carefully place a handful of flower pedals around the candle. You can also scatter a few of the flower petals around on the table or add a piece ribbon.

Materials needed:
3 adorn vases, 3 pillar candles, a box of flower petals, one yard of pretty white lace ribbon and some glass marbles.

our special day

This is a very simple centerpiece but it will add a lot of sparkle to any table.

Materials needed:
3 cylinder vases at different heights, 3 glass hanging votive cups, 3 white candle votives, 3 bags of clear acrylic gems, some white sand and a couple of white silk flowers.

This centerpiece is rather contemporary but elegant. Using different colored votives and marbles will make it coordinate with any wedding color scheme.

candle cubes

Materials needed:
one 10" square glass dinner plate, four 3" square glass votive holders, four small white votives, sqaure or round, small package of clear marble to put around the edge of the plate and one package of silver gravel.

votives in a row

This centerpiece is very simple and ideal for when you need something for any long narrow table. Nothing is more beautiful than a row of simple votives down the center of the table. Maybe you can add a few silver marbles around the votives. This will also add a little more sparkle to the table.

Materials needed:
6 to 8 flower pots or square votive holders, 6 to 8 white tea light votive candles, a handful of silver marbles, which is optional.

50

This is an inexpensive, eclectic centerpiece that you can have all your family and friends help you with. They can start by collecting old votives from garage and estate sales or flea markets. They can be very charming and unique. Add a little sand or glass chips in the bottom and put a small candle votive in each one and you are ready to go. You will need: 6 - 8 misc. glass votives, all sizes and shapes, 6 - 8 votive candles or tea light votives, some coarse white sand. Rock salt works great, too. Cluster them together for a unique look.

eclectic votives

wedding stemware collection

This is a great centerpiece for weddings or bridal showers because when the get-together is over, the bride and groom get to keep a set of stemware. Hopefully, you'll have at least 6 tables so they can have a service for six.
Place a dollop of hot wax under each votive to hold it in place.

You will need:
several wine glasses of various sizes for each table. One small candle votive to put on top of each piece of stemware. One bunch of silk flowers for inside each bowl, as shown in picture below.

bride & groom photo centerpiece

This is a wonderful centerpiece that is full of fond memories showcased on your reception table. You can use current bride and groom photos or photos of them as children, maybe even photos of your family. Just photo copy your pictures in a row and tape it on the glass piece as in the picture above. Trim with a pretty white lace ribbon. Fill with marbles and a white 6" pillar candle. Add a few small candle votives around the larger pieces and it is ready to go.

angela

This is a beautiful glass hurricane that is perfect with a simple floral candle ring placed under the hurricane filled with glass marbles and a 6" pillar candle. Simple and very elegant.

54

white lace

Contemporary and elegant, imagine this on your tables at your reception or bridal shower. You can find wonderful white lace at any fabric or craft store. The amount depends on the number and diameter of each glass cylinder jar.

holiday centerpieces

simple holiday décor

One of the most important rules I always tell my friends when decorating for the holidays: decorate to your taste and budget level and always pick a theme and stick to it. If you want your home to be spectacular, then don't try to do everything. A color coordinated home is tasteful and elegant and your friends and family will think you are a genius.

Another simple rule is to stick to what you can accomplish in a weekend. The holidays are to enjoy and celebrate with friends and family. Don't try to do too much to make your life crazy. (This is something that took me 20 years to understand and figure out.)

candle centerpiece

Here is one of the simplest holiday centerpieces ever!

Take any glass bowl, large vase or container and fill it with red and white marbles and place a beautiful red candle in the center. Cinnamon or cranberry scent is best for the holidays.

shiny ornaments

This is another simple centerpiece that I always use for the holidays.

Materials needed:
shiny ornaments, pine cones, cranberries, candy canes or glass balls.

holiday
harbour

What a simple way to celebrate the holidays. I've always stuck with traditional holiday colors of red and green, maybe adding a little gold or silver here and there, sometimes adding a glen plaid patter or colorful stripes. But shiny red ornaments, evergreen, pine cones and red ribbon just seem to say it all for me.

Materials needed:
2 straight sided footed glass hurricanes, some small pine cones or colored marbles, 2 - 6" pillar candles, 2 round glass plates and lots of evergreen branches, real or artificial. I always build my centerpiece on a plate or platter, so I can move it around without disturbing the arrangement.

four square votives

This holiday centerpiece is ideal for a fireplace mantle or the center of a buffet or dining room table. It's one of my favorites. Take any long glass or ceramic tray, place the votives down the center and fill in all around the votives with fresh evergreen, pine cones and cranberries. Most artificial greens will work as well.

This is a great centerpiece collection used almost anywhere in the house. I will have a set of them on my dining room buffet as well as one on the desk in the foyer.

holiday trio

snow scape

This centerpiece is very crisp and fresh looking. Spraying the snow can be a little difficult, but in the end you will love the sparkly winter look.

Materials needed: one angela hurricane, spray snow, 6" pillar candle, some silver artificial evergreen and some marbles or sand for the bottom of the hurricane vase.

silver bells

This beautiful landscaped collection of crystal vases filled with all sorts of sparkly holiday decorations is perfect for the holiday season. I love the look of white and silver along with some natural elements like pine cones and twigs.

cylinder candlesticks

These cylinder vases are filled with all sorts of wonderful artificial winter berries. They can be filled with evergreen, berries and pine cones or bright shiny ornaments or even colorful ribbons. Add the saucer and a pillar candle and you are ready to celebrate the holiday season.

young & modern

cool & crisp

Take three simple tall round vases of different heights and fill one of them with some decorative balls or glass balls. Fill the other two with some clear glass marbles or glass chips about half full and add a 6" or 8" pillar candle in the center of each vase.

aqua madness

What could be more sleek and beautiful than a centerpiece in your favorite colors of purple, violet and turquoise?

Materials needed:
3 vases, 2 about 11 or 12" tall and one 15" - 17" tall, lots of colored glass marbles or gems, several large colorful balls and two 6" pillar candles.

back to nature

The natural colors of brown make a very pleasing arrangement for today's home decor.

Materials needed:
various round cylinder vases of different heights and sizes, some natural twigs balls, berries, potpourri, reeds and a couple of pillar candles and holders. Mix it up. The more different the better.

cool trio

71

simply
gerbers

This centerpiece is ideal for sitting on a sofa table or the center of a dining room table. I like the simple symmetry of small vases lined up in a row.

electric silver

Sleek and contemporary, this black and silver centerpiece will be dramatic and dazzling when placed anywhere in your home. Use a few cylinder vases, a couple of candles and lots of silver and black marbles and rocks. Sometimes a few black marbles scattered on the table look great.

fun and festive

Bright cheerful colors will liven up any room in your home. I've chosen yellows, oranges and pinks, but a lot of other color combinations will work as well. Adding a band of ribbon will really help add a coordinated look to your centerpiece.

75

Here is an eclectic group of vases, filled with all
your favorite things. This is one of my favorites
because I love to collect all kinds of things. This
grouping is also easy to add to as your
collection grows.

decorative home

decorative accessories

When accessorizing your home, pick glass containers that go well with your furnishings. When you really want to shake things up, try something really unusual. But normally, do what you are comfortable with. In the long run you will probably be more satisfied.

Taking a simple large glass jar and fill it with shells, pine cones, sea glass or silk flowers will be a very easy way to add some simple decorations to your home.

The following few pages will show some wonderful glass pieces filled with simple things.

nature's terrarium

These are great when you live in the city with limited space or even at the office. You will need one very large glass ball or oversize glass container. The size depends on how large you want your tabletop garden to be and where you are going to put it.

Try using some stones and top soil, a plant or two and some rocks or small figurine.

vintage
collection

Before you get rid of all your old vases that are a mismatched collection, try putting them all together as a centerpiece. They can be filled with all the same things or different things in each vase. You'll be surprised how wonderful it will look. I've used a collection of vintage old buttons, old jewelry, marbles, music scrolls, wooden blocks, photographs and old silver spoons or utensils. You could also try using all your shells from that recent trip to Florida. What a wonderful way to display your most treasured or heirloom collectables.

seaside
paradise

Here is a wonderful collection of shells
that is timeless in its beauty. Use various
shells from your recent vacation or
purchase them in a retail store (tell your
friends you found them all on the beach).
No one will know the difference.

classic
collection

83

Nothing is as timeless and yet beautiful as old vintage memorabilia. Put it all in a variety of cylinder vases with a few candles and you have something that is a wonderful reminder of your past.

What could
be more
passionate
than a
centerpiece in
the wonderful
color pallet of
purples,
plums and
violet?

purple passion

84

I like to use a pair of these on my dining room table, but you can use one almost anywhere in the house. Change the colors and candle for each holiday or season.

85

square candlelights

craft ideas

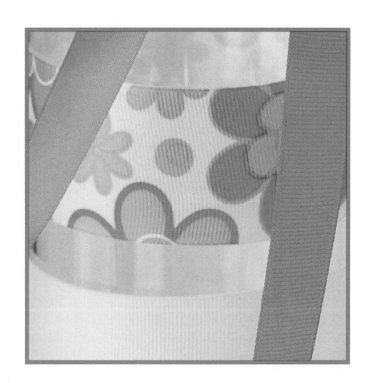

memory vases

This is another one of my favorites and can be adapted to a family reunion, bridal shower, wedding reception, birthday party or baby shower. It all depends on the photos you paste on the cylinder vases. It's not permanent, but looks great on the table for a centerpiece.

Take almost any glass vase and glue your favorite photos on each side or around. Cut the shape of the photos to fit your vase.

fun with ribbon

This may take a few extra minutes, but the results will be outstanding. Whether you use white ribbon for a wedding or bold colors for everyday, you will be pleasantly surprised at your own creativity.

89

candle carousel

This is a wonderful centerpiece for a bridal or baby shower. Use colored ribbon to match your theme. Here I've used two-sided tape to attached the ribbon to each piece of glass.

sparkle bling

This is a fun craft project. You will need a hot melt glue gun, lots of your favorite colored glass marbles that are flat on one side. Use almost any container that has flat sides. Put a small dollop of hot glue of the flat side of the glass marble and place it on the container. Hold it there for a few seconds until the glue cools. Repeat until the entire container is covered to your satisfaction. Add a pillar candle and you are all set. Or you can buy the self-adhesive gems that you just peel and stick. Either way, you end up with a vey sparkly centerpiece.

INDEX

About the author.

This is ROBERT ZOLLWEG's fourth book and his first on **Creative Accents** and decorating with glass for your home. His first three cookbooks were **Just Mini Desserts**, **Just Tastings** with mini appetizers, soups and salads and **Just Mini Cocktails**. All of these continue his passion for entertaining. He is a native of Toledo, Ohio and has been in the tabletop industry for almost 40 years. He designs glassware, flatware and ceramic products for the retail and foodservice industry and has worked with all of the major retailers including Walmart, Crate and Barrel, Williams-Sonoma, Macy's, Pier One Imports, Cost Plus World Market, Bed Bath & Beyond, JCPenneys, Target, Kohl's, Sears and Home Outfitters to name a few. Most of his professional career has been with Libbey Glass in Toledo, Ohio. He has traveled the world extensively looking for color and design trends and the right products to design and bring to the retail and foodservice marketplace.

Robert is also an artist-painter and works primarily with acrylic on canvas using bold primary colors. He currently lives in his home in Toledo's Historic Old West End and in the artistic community of Saugatuck, Michigan.

To find more information about Robert Zollweg, visit his web site at www.zollwegart.com

94

I hope you have enjoyed my book on decorating with **Creative Accents**. It should help you to decorate your home a little more creatively.

My cookbooks, **Just Mini Desserts** (quick and easy mini desserts) **Just Tastings** (mini appetizers, soups and salads) and **Just mini Cocktails**, are available at area retailers or on my web site.

www.zollwegart.com

Enjoy,
Robert

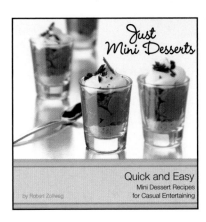